Resin in the Milky Way

Resin in the Milky Way
© Amanda Rabaduex / Cathexis Northwest Press

No part of this book may be reproduced without written permission of the
publisher or author, except in reviews and articles.

First Printing: 2024

ISBN: 978-1-952869-87-7

Editing & Design by C. M. Tollefson
Cathexis Northwest Press

cathexisnorthwestpress.com

Resin in the Milky Way

Poems
Amanda Rabaduex

Cathexis Northwest Press

For Love

Table of Contents

And Also With You — 1

Effing Love — 2

Anne Boleyn and Sylvia Plath Discuss Love — 4

when I think of Pompeii, I am full of longing — 5

maybe one day we'll drive to New Mexico and find ourselves in a wormhole — 6

fire wants to be wild — 7

It's okay to say the hurricane has an eye — 9

fleeting — 10

when words appear in black and white, it seems they have the answers — 11

years after we've stopped seeking each other's heat — 12

we once loved the sun — 14

what the water gave me — 15

"the secret is that the world loves you" waltz — 16

this is not what you need — 18

when my heart burns and death grows its own pulse — 21

To ▬▬▬▬▬▬ — 23

And Also With You

This is a poem
so already I can sense
that you want to back
away. Unless you're
one of my kind whose
heart busts open when
the sky is pink and who
looks at the stars and thinks
about all of humanity. And
if that's you, now you'll want
to stop reading because who
has time for all this sentimentality?
We have things to do. Longing
should be held on the tongue
like the melting body
of Christ. Give it a
dark wet cave and
keep it to yourself,
all the ways you hope
it will save you. How
you really just showed up
to drink the blood.

Effing Love

It started with a stranger, a sailor
his face looked like me – like a sea.
I called his name from the edge
but all he heard was wind.
It was Jupiter I turned to,
red storm raging.
It's always men
who like to watch a woman
drown in the river,
like to touch the torch
to the stake,
that do it for me.
The ones who summon my middle name,
whisper ways we could evade prayer
before the center unravels.
Trade coins for candy,
carry the Pacific in our eyelashes,
breathe in so deep,
we pull Texas into our lungs.
This is not a metaphor.
It is the way I sail
unceasingly around the sun.
Wrapped in plumeria on a beach,
conch to my ear,
I thought I heard an ocean,
but it was air
trapped   vibrating.
He ran a finger along places
destined to be my future
scars, explained how we had been
split apart.   Something about
Plato.   Something about
the broken clock made me believe
the myth. His words – velvet abyss,
a sky drooping low.
September grew cold.
Who would try to hold on

to a body, anyway?
These remnants of broken stars,
scraps the light has forgotten.
In space, galaxies are pulled
towards black holes –
not the smile in his eyes.
I said yes.
A vow spiraling around the shell.
I wanted to be in something.
I was always the water.
He was always the moon
pushing into me
trying to find the place
I've hidden God.
But she's already moved on.
Sick of being the excuse for blood
& sex & poetry.
She is not waiting.
We keep thinking of ways to fail ourselves.
I keep thinking of ways
to convince him
I can carry his ship to shore.
Convince him –
these breasts,
these hips,
these words
would sink.

Anne Boleyn and Sylvia Plath Discuss Love

Have you ever seen eyes the color of rain sitting atop a window? There are windows so thick the sky is a blur. He spoke to me once like I'd conjured a winter sunrise. I bit his cheek as hard as I could but I choked on the copper taste of blood. I never felt how deep my teeth could sink, how quickly I would swallow after I'd chewed. Metal is something that is never forgotten. A glint that blinds the eye. Beliefs in love and sex and God can be bought. What does it feel like for a man to sever the body, separate lips from hands? Prayer becomes impossible. What does it feel like to hold breath the way I hold love? Tea without honey. Fog settling on the road. The sound of a whetstone. Was it sharp? Yes. Until the clock spun backwards, I'd never wanted. Never wanted anything more.

when I think of Pompeii,
I am full of longing

who can help wanting to hold on
to a moment
 capture it in light
 until it sears the skin
     statuesque, the last breath
we lie down on our edges
     floating orbs
        the center does not burn
           like yearning
no, the center will not hold
              it will dig fingernails into its own palms
            crying   out
truth   is   a breathless release

                              I love

                                            thin walls
                             how easily a house is buried
                              & a body becomes stone
                        like it was never meant to be
             a structure temporary   a soft story
                         cleaved into grass until
                    the roof begins to rot   sun
                too hot rain too heavy world too
                                      unsteady
                             we are

running from the river
all we'll know of forever   we are
running   in place   we are
                                              ruined

maybe one day we'll drive to New Mexico and find ourselves in a wormhole

there is beauty
  under the covers
where we keep
  the light out

forbidden places
in the center
  of my sigh

I don't want
  to need gravity
I only want
  the way you look at me

maybe we aren't meant to
  exit the highway

hypnotic spin
  of a world that never stops

what is God thinking

we'll just cruise along in the heat
  over the plateau

fire wants to be wild

how I love to watch the sky burn

& pretend heaven isn't
    mostly empty

stars are small here
    infinite bodies
  consuming their own inferno
and we sleep

every atom is a shrouded world
we should be suspicious

look at silence – it has secrets
    every seed a tree
      every tree a forest fire

every day the moon leaves
this is how it will always be –
  a light kiss in the night
    and by morning – abandoned
      glaring dawn and clouds

   they say if sound
could move through space
our sun would break us
like frantic ringing of
a trillion cathedrals
a schism

from branches of the dying oak,
crows study me

would I trade
fingers for flight

consider hands   how they hold on

    how they need
          softly
      caress the church of the body
        beckon the silent *almost* of God

a lamp turns midnight to noon
but no walls can hold onto the light

I fill the air with what I'm not saying

can you see it?

        the room is dark

               the flame jumps

black feathers
        float

     down

It's okay to say the hurricane has an eye

but if I call tree branches arms
that are reaching out, I'm stuck
in a romantic era. The truth is

I'm looking for a truce—
I'll take an olive branch,

or the fruit
of a whole orchard.

Wind blows the willow
into a green ocean ready
to help me get carried
away. I'm learning how

to let go of the idea of embrace,
learning to see the trees—
needy, knee deep, needing
to push their most delicate parts

into dirt while all that can be seen
is how they grow towards the sun,

& now I've done it again –
found splinters of God
everywhere I look
like a storm-shattered oak.

If only my eye were a calm center.

I'm not wrong to say *love*
when the trees breathe us in

fleeting

forget the void
forget broken in two
skin   a continuum
we are scared   sacred
prayerful unbelievers
lips intersect in confessing

sin of my skin, your psalms
help me forget to remember
the certain song

your head carries all the words
that make a world
but when I hold your face in my hands
I hear just one –

– press my tongue
into your wind
scattering dead leaves
the flavor is ephemeral

our heaviness ripples the dark silk
of space
as deep inside as we'll ever be

the water is water
green leaves are turning red

years after we've stopped seeking each other's heat

we turn on the t.v.
                the wildman appears
                    barefoot
                                  shouting
      hucklebuck
                pulling

pythons from swamps
                      in the Everglades

I can't look away

when the world turns cold   we coil
                                like snakes
              under bushes

curl into the self
                      hide
in the trunk of the dead
                tree   waiting
for spring   until

warmth surprises
            grabs from behind,
                      stretches
                body
shining
      under the headlight

the python turns
    to strike
            but now his hand
                    is around her neck   and she

when words appear in black and white, it seems they have the answers

                while I have fallen
              into the gray
         in-betweenness of it all
             found a home
                in a body
                   that walks itself
                            towards the fire
                but cowers from ash
       turns away from the tiger
           lilies' orange growl
               coiled goldenrod
                         pull the flowers
                  from my hand
                    & I feel
              the sway
          of my own hips
          how the heart relearns
                 rhythm
                      under a cloud
                    pouring
      itself onto skin
              love becomes
           slippery
             middle
                to dissolve
                  the taste of holding on
       and letting go
                I have fallen
                    into the no thing
              of everything

is his
        she knows it
                she gives in
                        her body stretched   no longer holding on and he
is excited
      by each soft pound   her whole life
has led to this
              devouring each moment
of deer, herons, alligators   growing
                                  into what he's been looking for
                    she's the one
his record-breaker   soon
      he will rip her open   her skin
              will be massaged
        into something he wraps around himself
every step he takes
                she'll be moving with him

        across our living room
            I see your face
                    lost behind the screen of your phone
                          I feel myself coil in this cold
                        the only hope
                            is for summer
                            to return

we once loved the sun

a bluebird returns
    to its nest
thin worm in its beak

I pass a pasture emptied
    of cattle   replaced with rows
of modular homes &

streetlamps   now we see
    no stars   nothing
to wish upon

what a world   we try to love
    every moment flies back
holding some shriveled thing

I cling   in the morning
    shadows   how
they carry darkness weightlessly

birdsong pushes towards sky
    can't raise it high enough
clouds collapse on the mountain peak

remember how I followed you
    like there were no horizons?
how I held dawn?   palms burning

what the water gave me

after Florence + the Machine & Frida Kahlo

raindrops on a forehead
a melting crown
an old god in the clouds
lightning striking an eel
jealousy
the end of a forest fire
width of the ocean
a metaphor
weaponized body
        a woman in the river
        is always a witch
        fear is why they build arks
rusted knives
horizon as a tarnished line
        this is how to unite sea and sky
                it's always a lie
becoming undone by the rings in a puddle
the center of a hurricane
        is an eye
the center of an eye
        is a black hole
        waiting for light
this body
        I must carry around the sun
a taste for drowning

"the secret is that the world loves you" waltz

-after Kelli Russell Agodon

in early morning's quiet
        rays murmur through the window
warm lines on my thighs

        my skin so in love with heat
I'd kiss the sun if I could
        how can we hold what we can't grasp?

at night in the valley
        winter's silence is shunned
shadows rustle last year's leaves

        an owl keeps asking *who*
the cold snaps its teeth
        I've swallowed so much dirt

I know the taste of endings
        when the tongue is tender, it will bleed
there's a secret language with peace

        lilies, leaves wilt like weeping
a need to drink the light
        cocktail of radiation

I found a puzzle of seasons
        unblemished wings
it took three days to assemble

        & thirty nine years
to piece together the world
        into questions I could not answer

now I'm trying to tear it apart
        put it back in the closet
sometimes we want it to storm

        sound is never loud enough
we want to hear clouds crash
        like symbols in a symphony

like the rage of a sea knocking at the door
        waves invisible
shaking arms of trees

        it's almost like this world
is flooded with confessions
        that we're never ready to believe

this is not what you need

> *"Our lives do not correspond to this fanciful completion that is represented by sentences, which is, of course, why we love sentences, why we love novels, because it gives us what we can't have. Poetry, I think, gives us what we do have, which is the sense of fragmentation and incompletion."* - Philip Brady

you want
what you can't have

a place where the swan swimming
                               on the lake
foreshadows
         the man jumping
off a cold bridge

                     it could be any swan   any jump

the point is you want the last page

the point is you want to carry the entire story
to live
          within & beyond it

      you seek the confines of an edge
the way a whetstone seeks a knife

      you hate today

resent the mundane of too many nows
now the grocery store is crowded
now bologna's on sale, a 53 cent decrease
in aisle three next to flea & tick treatments
you think of backstory, fatal flaws

you think in the denouement,
the man could have lived
                   you are glad he took the plunge
      you feel bad you don't feel bad

now you catch every red light driving to an empty library
now you wonder if the pacing was just right
  could he have stared at churning water
 just a while longer
maybe while puffing American Spirit

      you ignore the typo on page 604
     some things get overlooked; it's life – even editors
    get pink eye

the faucet dripping into the sink
sounds like time looking over our shoulder

each sunset
  one more day we don't have
a reason for being
mornings are a ceaseless spiraling into tomorrows

alarm clock sounding the same revolution
    & we are not a hero on a journey
   not even when we stand on the southern tip of Chile

no ship, no yellow Mustang, no wolf tracks, no space chase gold mine collapse white water rafting magic ring volcano demon bear deterring tossing keys to the valet with a Benjamin & a wink

you still think
your name means   God's gift
but it's just a whiplash of busses to Brooklyn,
basic sedans crossing bridges
to the place we have to reach
blank boilerplate
vanilla vanilla burrow bromidic city

      you think what you want is what you need
I agree–
you deserve a fanciful completion:

```
                        you
            sin
            sal
                you                    desert sky
                            you
            olive branch
                    unthink
        you             tú          too         con
                                                sol

                you

        (but you will never find it)
```

when my heart burns and death grows its own pulse

I think of the words of mine
you'll find
when I'm gone

It will seem I thought a lot
about sunsets full moons and trees
& I did

but one day you'll see:
a mock orange breeze
will blow against your cheek

& you'll think of the ways you tried
not to be afraid
the way you placed yourself

in an open palm
& ran singing through the spaces
between rain drops

despite
despite
the way you were pulled

by love
like a glowing satellite
like the dark pit of a cherry

cradled in sweetness, falling
toward the ground
you'll see the depths of the ocean

in the eyes of your children
&, son, that is when
you'll look up

wonder where all
this light is going,
how to hold it

& what we ever did
to deserve the soft unfurling
of all these shimmering leaves

To ▮▮▮▮▮▮▮▮▮▮▮▮

after Julia De Burgos

when you say that you are like the dust rising,
the way it makes real lines of the sun's rays

I know you are lying
it isn't existence you see

but the way it crumbles into fragments
yesterday's quiet fermata

you are breathing in the wilted orchard
you are inhaling an orange eaten last week

you are trying to piece the skin back together
and when you can't, you shake

like you intended to fade
but you remember the sky

is something we never grasp
even 10,000 feet up

with the door open
it was called jumping

it was called free fall
though there is nothing free

about returning to the ground,
its inevitability

when you say you have loved
I know you don't know its depths

how one day the mouth opens for the last time
its emptiness no longer yours to fill

there are only so many days to say
I

never knowing how to count the light
or how much of the sun to claim for ourselves

one day you will become the blush of the morning
some window will be lifted

skin will grow into a new home
curled between roots of a swaying willow

and *I* becomes a resin in the Milky Way
somewhere between the written lines

Some of these poems were previously published, some under different titles or different form, in the following publications:

> "fire wants to be wild"
> *Fahmidan Journal*
>
> "'the secret is that the world loves you' waltz"
> *Solstice Literary Magazine*
>
> "what the water gave me"
> *Barren Magazine*

Amanda Rabaduex is a poet, writer, editor, and educator. She served in the Air Force and taught yoga prior to earning a BA and an MA in English and an MA in Poetry, and an MFA in Creative Writing from Wilkes University.

Her poetry has been nominated for Best of the Net and a Pushcart Prize. Originally from Ohio, she lives near Knoxville, Tennessee.

Also Available from Cathexis Northwest Press:

Something To Cry About
by Robert Krantz

Suburban Hermeneutics
by Ian Cappelli

God's Love Is Very Busy
by David Seung

that one time we were almost people
by Christian Czaniecki

Fever Dream/Take Heart
by Valyntina Grenier

The Book of Night & Waking
by Clif Mason

Dead Birds of New Zealand
by Christian Czaniecki

The Weathering of Igneous Rockforms in High-Altitude Riparian Environments
by John Belk

If A Fish
by George Burns

How to Draw a Blank
by Collin Van Son

En Route
by Jesse Wolfe

sky bright psalms
by Temple Cone

Moonbird
by Henry G. Stanton

southern athiest. oh, honey
by d. e. fulford

Bruises, Birthmarks & Other Calamities
by Nadine Klassen

Wanted: Comedy, Addicts
by AR Dugan

They Curve Like Snakes
by David Alexander McFarland

the catalog of daily fears
by Beth Dufford

Shops Close Too Early
by Josh Feit

Vanity Unfair and Other Poems
by Robert Eugene Rubino

Destructive Heresies
by Milo E. Gorgevska

Bodies of Separation
by Chim Sher Ting

The Night with James Dean and Other Prose Poems
by Allison A. deFreese

About Time
by Julie Benesh

Suspended
by Ellen White Rook

The Unempty Spaces Between
by Louis Efron

Quomodo probatur in conflatorio
by Nick Roberts

Suspended
by Ellen White Rook

Call Me Not Ishmael but the Sea
by J. Martin Daughtry

Wild Evolution
by Naomi Leimsider

Coming To Terms
by Peter Sagnella

Acta
by Patrick Wilcox

Honeymoon Shoes
by Valyntina Grenier

Practising Ascending
by Nadine Hitchiner

Home Visit
by Michal Rubin

LA CIUDAD EN TI: THE CITY WITHIN YOU
by Karla Marrufo
Translated from the Spanish by Allison A. deFreese

Cathexis Northwest Press

www.ingramcontent.com/pod-product-compliance
Lightning Source LLC
Chambersburg PA
CBHW020443090526
44586CB00045B/835